This book belongs to

_____

_____
Date

To Andy, and our shared fight for joy.
—BBS

For all my sisters—those best friends who came biologically, those who my brothers were wise enough to snag, and those who came through blessed life crossings. You are a gift.
—MK

To my sweet daughters, Starr and Summer.
—KP

Text © 2015 McArthur Krishna and Bethany Brady Spalding

Illustrations © 2015 Kathleen Peterson

Art direction by Richard Erickson
Design by Shauna Gibby

All rights reserved. No part of this book may be reproduced in any form or by any means without permission in writing from the publisher, Deseret Book Company, at permissions@deseretbook.com or P. O. Box 30178, Salt Lake City, Utah 84130. This work is not an official publication of The Church of Jesus Christ of Latter-day Saints. The views expressed herein are the responsibility of the authors and do not necessarily represent the position of the Church or of Deseret Book Company.

DESERET BOOK is a registered trademark of Deseret Book Company.

Visit us at DeseretBook.com

Library of Congress Cataloging-in-Publication Data

Krishna, McArthur, author.
  Girls Who Choose God: stories of strong women from the Book of Mormon / McArthur Krishna and Bethany Brady Spalding; illustrated by Kathleen Peterson.
      pages cm
   Includes bibliographical references.
   ISBN 978-1-62972-101-9 (hardbound : alk. paper)
1. Women in the Book of Mormon—Juvenile literature. 2. Book of Mormon—Biography—Juvenile literature. I. Spalding, Bethany Brady, author. II. Peterson, Kathleen B., 1951– illustrator. III. Title.
BX8627.3.K75 2015
289.3'2209252—dc23   2015017118

Printed in China   06/2015
R. R. Donnelley, Shenzhen, China

10 9 8 7 6 5 4 3 2 1

Girls Who Choose God
Stories of Strong Women from the Book of Mormon

McARTHUR KRISHNA • BETHANY BRADY SPALDING
ILLUSTRATED BY KATHLEEN PETERSON

Salt Lake City, Utah

In painting these scenes from the Book of Mormon, I hoped to convey two important concepts: First, the love of God blesses all of us. The tree of life in Lehi's dream is a representation of God's love (see 1 Nephi 11:21–22), and each story opens with an image of a native Mesoamerican tree to reflect that love. Second, the Savior taught, "by their fruits ye shall know them" (3 Nephi 14:20). All of these trees are fruit bearing, reminding us that we come to know these women by the exemplary choices they made.

Kathleen

Girls Who Choose God
Stories of Strong Women from the Book of Mormon

Women in the Book of Mormon are powerful models of choosing God. When we discovered these women's stories for ourselves, we wanted to herald their extraordinary acts of faith to others. We believed families would be inspired by the choices these women made. Book of Mormon women chose to defend their families, protect their husbands, risk their lives for others, and live for peace. They chose to learn about the magnificence of God's plan and then taught truth to their children and others.

We personally feel it is vital for Latter-day Saints to learn about and celebrate the women in the Book of Mormon. Over 150 passages have "explicit references to women, offering an exciting bundle of information about our fore-sisters in the gospel."[1] Their stories highlight that women, whether as individuals or part of a group, used their agency to be active participants in God's work. The scriptures often don't tell us their names, but they tell us what they did—and these women's brave choices should be honored.

Women's choices impact the entire human family. As Elder M. Russell Ballard said, "As we look for and find women in our scriptures and in our history, we will see far better the power and influence women have on family, community, the Church, and the world." He further encouraged, "We need to develop the skill to find their influence."[2] We wrote this book with the intent of helping families develop the skill of seeing and emulating strong women.

In telling these stories, we have been true to the scriptures while also ascribing natural human emotion and attributes and drawing logical conclusions. We feel the Book of Mormon gives sufficient information about these strong women to "bless our lives through their examples and teachings."[3] Regardless of how much we know about them, God knows and loves them—and each of us—individually, distinctly, and perfectly.

May these women's stories inspire all of us to choose God.

Bethany and McArthur

---

1. Marjorie Meads Spencer, "My Book of Mormon Sisters," *Ensign,* Sept. 1977, 66–71.
2. "Righteous Women Essential to God's Work, Elder Ballard Says," *Church News,* May 4, 2015.
3. Dieter F. Uchtdorf, "The Influence of Righteous Women," *Ensign,* Sept. 2009, 5.

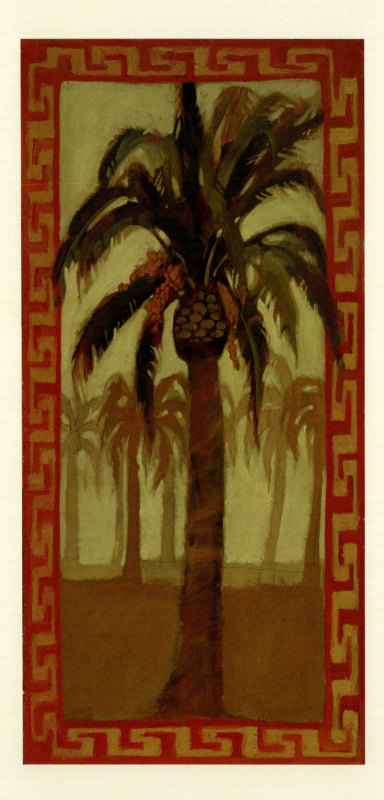

Sariah, the Matriarch

Sariah was a goodly parent. She and her husband, Lehi, nurtured each of their children and taught them many important truths. Despite their efforts, two of their sons struggled to believe in God. When Sariah's family left Jerusalem for the wilderness, Laman and Lemuel made many poor choices that hurt themselves and others. Their hearts were hard.

Sariah had a choice to make. She could give up on Laman and Lemuel,

or

she could continue to love and lead all of her children. . . .

Sariah chose to love unconditionally. Even though she grieved over Laman and Lemuel's actions, she tried to encourage them. As the wise matriarch of her family, she counseled her children and reminded them that God had protected them. Regardless of her sons' choices, Sariah tried to love them as God loves. Sariah's wisdom and love influenced generations. Her children were among those who settled the promised land, and many of her descendants were visited by Jesus Christ.

When have you chosen to love unconditionally?

1 Nephi 1:1; 5:8; 18:17–18

A Strong Wife Calls on God

Nephi's wife was strong. As part of Ishmael's family, she left her home in Jerusalem and ventured into the desert to join Sariah and Lehi's clan. After marrying Nephi, she gave birth in the wilderness. And even though she had only raw meat to eat, she was still able to breastfeed and care for her babies. Her strength helped her overcome the many hardships of journeying in the wilderness and crossing the ocean. While on the ship, Nephi's brothers, Laman and Lemuel, became angry with him and bound him with cords.

Nephi's wife had a choice to make. She could stand back and watch Laman and Lemuel hurt Nephi,

or

she could use her spiritual strength to ask God to protect her husband. . . .

Confronting Laman and Lemuel, Nephi's wife cried for his life. The callous brothers refused to release him, so she turned to God in mighty prayer. God created a great tempest that tossed their ship for four days. Frightened, Laman and Lemuel released Nephi. The power of God had softened their hearts. Nephi's wife's prayers were answered.

When have you chosen to use your strengths for good?

1 Nephi 7:1–5, 19; 16:7; 17:1–2; 18:12–14, 19–20

Sisters at a Crossroads

The sisters of Nephi, Laman, and Lemuel loved their family. But the fighting between their brothers was fierce. After arriving in the promised land, their mother and father died and no one could keep the peace. Their younger brother, Nephi, had been called by God as the prophet. Laman and Lemuel were angry because they followed the tradition that the oldest brother should be in charge. To protect Nephi, God warned him to flee into the wilderness with everyone who wanted to go. The sisters loved all their brothers, and it must have pained them to see their family torn apart.

The sisters had a choice to make. They could follow tradition and stay with their older brothers,

or

they could break from tradition to follow God. . . .

The sisters "believed in the warnings and the revelations of God" and chose to unite with the prophet—their brother Nephi. Taking their tents and all they could carry, they journeyed in the wilderness for many days. The people created a new community where they strived to follow the teachings of God. They tended the land as they raised animals, planted seeds, and reaped rich harvests. Crafting gold, silver, and copper, they built an exceedingly fine temple to worship God. The sisters and their families grew and God blessed them abundantly.

When have you chosen to break from false tradition to follow God?

2 Nephi 5:4–7, 11, 15–17

Women Who Clapped for Joy

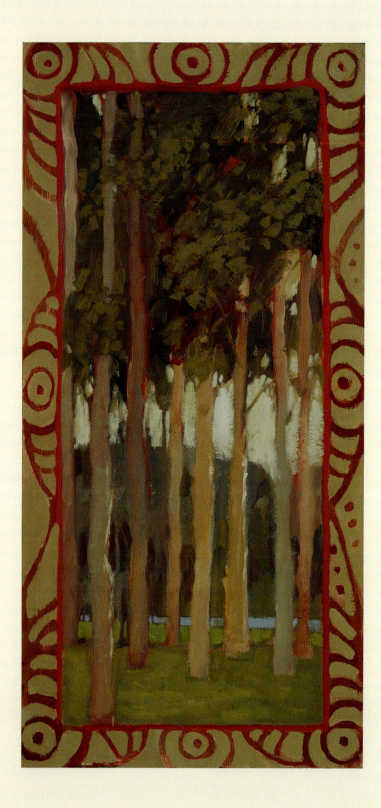

Many women and men were eager to learn more about God's plan for them. A priest named Alma wanted to share God's great plan of happiness with everyone, but the vicious King Noah was threatening his life. Anyone who wanted to learn about God had to meet in secret. Though it was dangerous, hundreds of people snuck into the forest to listen to Alma. Gathered around a pool of pure water, women, men, and children heard beautiful lessons about faith, repentance, and redemption. They learned that if they were willing to bear one another's burdens and stand as witnesses of God, they could each make a covenant with God through baptism.

The women had a choice to make. They could decide it was too risky to be a believer,

or

they could be brave and be baptized. . . .

Clapping their hands for joy, the women and all the people said, "This is the desire of our hearts." In the waters of Mormon, Alma baptized two hundred and four souls who believed. However, the king learned of their gathering and was angry. He sent his army to punish them, but the believers escaped into the wilderness with their families. As they built a new life and established a church, the believers cared for one another, helped those in need, and gave thanks to God. Their hearts were knit together in love.

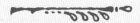

When have you been brave for your beliefs?

Mosiah 18:1–17, 21, 22, 34–35

The Heroic Daughters

The daughters from the land of Zeniff were very heroic. When a ferocious army attacked, the girls and their families were forced to flee their homes. As the army chased them, some fathers abandoned their families to save themselves. But many devoted fathers stayed. Realizing their families were about to be destroyed, the fathers turned to their daughters and caused them to plead with the soldiers.

The girls had a choice to make. They could try to escape,

or

they could listen to their fathers and confront the army, hoping to save their families. . . .

The courageous girls knew they were their families' only chance. With everyone they loved depending on them, the girls stood forth and pleaded with the fierce army. When the soldiers saw the girls, they listened to them, felt compassion, and stopped fighting. The army made an agreement that if the people surrendered half of their possessions, they could go back to their lands in peace. The girls had saved their families.

When have you placed the needs of your family above your own?

Mosiah 19:9–15

A Lamanite Queen of Great Faith

A Lamanite queen ruled with her husband, King Lamoni. One day, a missionary named Ammon arrived in their land. Ammon began to teach the king about God's love and mercy. When the king heard these truths, light filled his soul! His joy was so intense that he collapsed. After the king lay completely still for two days, the queen became worried. Some people thought he was dead and wanted to bury him, but the queen wasn't sure what to do.

The queen had a choice to make. She could give up her husband for dead,

or

she could ask God's servant Ammon for help. . . .

Exercising her faith, the queen asked Ammon to come and see her husband. Ammon explained to her that the king was not dead and promised he would rise again the next day. Ammon asked the queen if she believed his promise. Though she didn't fully understand Ammon's teachings, she still believed him. Ammon said, "Blessed art thou because of thy exceeding faith; I say unto thee, woman, there has not been such great faith among all the people of the Nephites." The queen's incredible faith was rewarded when her husband awoke the next day.

When have you chosen to have faith?

Alma 18:24–43; 19:1–13

Abish, the Daring Missionary

Abish was a young servant to the Lamanite queen. She had been taught by her father to believe in God, though no one in her community believed the same. Then God called a missionary named Ammon to teach the Lamanites the truths Abish already knew. When the queen and king heard these truths, their hearts swelled with joy. The Spirit was so strong that the queen, king, and Ammon fainted. When the royal servants saw this spectacle, they were overcome and fell to the earth. But Abish did not fear! She knew it was the power of God that had caused them to collapse.

Abish had a choice to make. She could keep her understanding of God a secret,

or

she could boldly invite her people to witness the power of God. . . .

Hoping for her people to believe, Abish ran from house to house inviting others to come and see the queen and king. Many people were curious and quickly gathered at the palace. When the multitude found their queen and king lying on the ground, they began to argue about what had caused this scene. In front of the entire crowd, Abish touched the queen's hand, and she immediately awoke. The queen stood up, praising God with a loud voice. Rejoicing, she reached for her husband's hand and raised him from the ground, too. Seeing these miracles, many people believed in God. Abish's bold missionary efforts helped to change the hearts of her people.

When have you invited someone to hear gospel truths?

Alma 18:24–43; 19:13–36

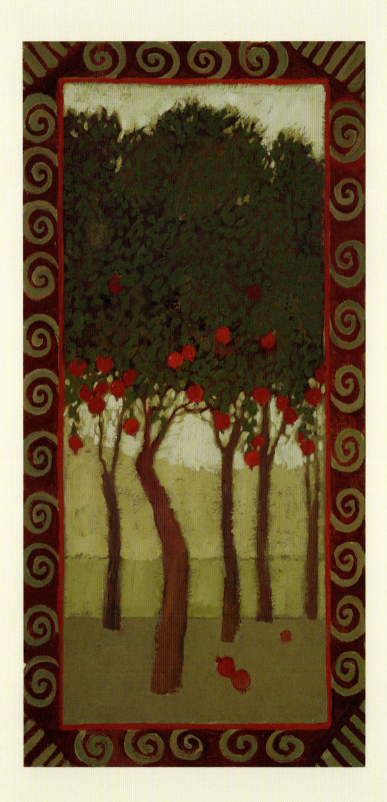

The Maidservant Spy

A young girl was a servant to a greedy leader named Morianton. He wanted more land, so he convinced his people to steal their neighbors' property. Captain Moroni was responsible for keeping the peace, so he and his soldiers set out to catch Morianton. But Morianton crafted a plan to escape. One night an angry Morianton beat the maidservant, who knew of his plan.

The maidservant had a choice to make. She could remain silent and live in fear,

or

she could share her knowledge with Moroni to help capture Morianton. . . .

Risking Morianton's wrath, the maidservant fled to Moroni's camp. She told Moroni about her beating and revealed the details of Morianton's escape plan. Using the maidservant's information, Moroni's army caught Morianton and his people. In the battle, Morianton was killed and his people were taken captive. But after they promised to live peacefully, Moroni allowed them to return to their homes. The maidservant had helped bring peace to the land and also to her own life.

When have you chosen to speak up against something that was wrong?

Alma 50:25–36

Mothers of the Stripling Warriors

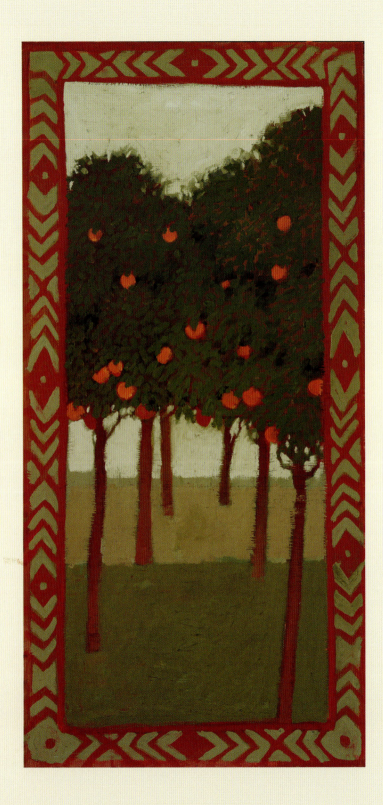

The Anti-Nephi-Lehi mothers were women of integrity. In the past, their people had been warlike. But after learning about Jesus Christ, they experienced a mighty change of heart. Burying all their weapons in a deep pit, the women and men made a covenant with God—promising to never fight again. For many years the Anti-Nephi-Lehies lived in peace. The mothers taught their children to trust God. They showed their children how to be true to God in all things. But now war raged through the land, and their families were in great danger.

The mothers had a choice to make. They could dig up their weapons and defend their families,

or

they could honor their covenant to never fight again. . . .

The mothers and fathers decided they would rather die than break their covenant with God. However, their children had been too young to make that covenant. Empowered by their mothers' faith, the sons offered to fight on behalf of their people. Helaman led them into battle, and though many were injured, not one of them died. The sons had been taught by their mothers that God would deliver them. The sons said, "We do not doubt our mothers knew it."

When have you chosen to keep a promise?

Alma 23:6–7, 16–17; 24:12–27; 53:10–21; 56:44–48, 55–56

Girls and Boys Blessed by Jesus

Many worried families sought refuge at the temple after a great destruction had ravaged the land. As the people gathered, a small voice spoke from heaven—piercing their souls and causing their hearts to burn. Looking up, the families saw a man in brilliant white robes descending from heaven. Stretching out His arms to the people, He said, "I am Jesus Christ. . . . I am the light and the life of the world." The resurrected Jesus invited everyone to come and feel the prints of the nails in His hands and feet. He explained how they too could be a light to the world. After teaching, Jesus asked that the children be brought to Him.

Each girl and boy had a choice to make. They could shy away,

or

they could gladly go to Jesus. . . .

Jesus was so warm and loving, the girls and boys willingly went with their parents to be with Him. When the children had circled around Him, Jesus blessed each girl and boy one by one. He prayed to God for them and tenderly wept. Jesus said to the people, "Behold your little ones." As they looked, the heavens opened and radiant angels lit up the sky. Encircling the children with fire, the angels ministered to them. Jesus' joy was full.

When have you chosen to come to Christ?

3 Nephi 11:1–11; 17:11–24

Choose God

Strong women in the Book of Mormon show us many ways to boldly choose God. Learning from their examples, we can gain strength for our own lives. We can love those who are different than us, speak out against wrongs, defend those in trouble, break from false traditions, and choose God in all things.

Be strong.

Family Discussion Questions

The questions found earlier in the book are designed to encourage children to reflect on their own lives and share specific examples. The expansive questions below are intended to generate ongoing conversations between all members of the family. We hope exploring these questions together will nurture a deeper understanding of God's truths.

Sariah, the Matriarch

- Why do you think God asks us to love each other?
- What does it mean to love unconditionally?
- Why can it sometimes be difficult to love our family members?
- How can we forgive family members when they hurt our feelings?

A Strong Wife Calls on God

- How does God sometimes bless our lives with unexpected paths?
- How do we balance relying on our own efforts and asking God for help?
- How does calling on God strengthen your relationship with God and change who you are?
- Why does God want wives and husbands to work together as "equal partners," as revealed in the Proclamation on the Family? What does that look like?

Sisters at a Crossroad

- What are some of the false traditions of our day?
- Why is it difficult to ignore culture and traditions?
- How can you build new traditions that bring you and your family closer to God?

Women Who Clapped for Joy

- What is one part of the gospel that makes you happy?
- Why do you (or did you) want to be baptized?
- What does it mean to mourn with those who mourn and comfort those who stand in need of comfort?

The Heroic Daughters

- Why did God place us in families?
- How do you know when to take care of yourself and when to put your family's needs first?
- How does each member of your family feel recognized and appreciated?

The Lamanite Queen of Great Faith

- How do you decide who or what to believe?
- How do we recognize truth?
- What does it mean to have a relationship with God?

Abish, the Daring Missionary

- What is one truth that blesses your life? How?
- How could you help another person understand that truth and the blessings it brings?
- Why can it be difficult to share your beliefs?

The Maidservant Spy

- Why are we sometimes afraid to make the right choice?
- How can God help you overcome fear?
- How can you turn something bad into something good?

Mothers of the Stripling Warriors

- What do you think are the most important things to teach children?
- What valuable lessons have you learned from your mother's example or from another mother?
- Why are mothers such powerful teachers?

Girls and Boys Blessed by Jesus

- How can you feel Jesus near you even though you don't see Him?
- Why do we sometimes resist coming closer to Jesus?
- What would you like to ask Jesus if you could sit with Him?